NIGHT TRAINS OF BRITISH RAIL

Alan Whitehouse

For Liz,

who gave up her evenings to tramp around endless railway platforms and sidings, popping flashgun, chatting up traincrew and getting reporting numbers for the captions. And who, seven months pregnant, stumbled around Glasgow's Mossend Yard on what should have been a holiday! I will always be grateful.

Published by Mainline & Maritime Ltd,
3 Broadleaze, Upper Seagry, near Chippenham, Wiltshire, SN15 5EY
www.mainlineandmaritime.co.uk - orders@mainlineandmaritime.co.uk - 01275 845012

ISBN: 978-1-900340-26-7

Front Cover: Shortly after midnight, activity on the Speedlink network was at its height, with trains pausing only at key locations to detach and attach short 'cuts' of wagons which have either come from, or will join, other Speedlink trains to give greater flexibility and a better customer offer. In Sheffield's Tinsley Yard, 47 174 waits with the 6E30 service.

Title Page: Perhaps the most famous overnight train of them all was the Irish Mail service which carried a mix of postal traffic and sleeper cars between London and Holyhead for the onward ferry connection to Ireland. Train headboards were out of fashion, but 1D84 was still 'named' in the BR timetable in 1982. It stands at Euston with 86 321 at the head.

Rear Cover: In the last years of the Travelling Post Office network, Royal Mail ran a train between Dover and Manchester. On this occasion, the Class 47 locomotive had recently been outshopped in the new 'large logo' livery.

Introduction

Taking a camera out in the hours of darkness to photograph trains is, on the face of it, an act of folly. For a start, it is dark and photographs are usually associated with good lighting. What is there to photograph? Do trains still run by night?

Well, it is still true that Britain's railway system never sleeps: there is always activity of some sort across a wide section of the network. But the trains that run today are few in number and, arguably less colourful and interesting than the night services that plied the network 30 0r 40 years ago, when the pictures in this book were taken.

Today, just two sleeper services leave Euston for Scotland (they split to serve five destinations) and a single train leaves Paddington for Penzance, reaching between them a relative handful of towns and cities. What a contrast with the 1970s when you could catch a sleeper from places as diverse as Barrow-in-Furness, Leeds, Newcastle, Cardiff and Holyhead – and vice-versa from London of course.

There was even a cross-country sleeper service linking Edinburgh and Bristol and, within Scotland so-called 'internal' sleeper services ran between Inverness, Glasgow and Edinburgh.

And they were far from alone. At the same time that the sleeping car staff were preparing their trains, shunters and locomotive crew would be assembling trains of newspaper and parcels vans. Post Office sorters would be making their way to the travelling post office trains which, at the time, were seen as the most important trains on the network: they were given priority over everything else to ensure as far as possible that every connection was made at every stopping point by every postal train. They were also always the first trains to be plotted on the graphs from which both working and public timetables are derived.

Like the postal services, newspaper trains were Class One traffic – the same priority as an express passenger train. And like postal trains it was vital that all connections at all calling points were maintained. Otherwise the overnight distribution system broke down.

In addition to helping to maintain the fabric of the nation, these trains had an enduring fascination for railway followers and enthusiasts. In the 1970s and 80s when newer stock was displacing some of the Modernisation Plan locomotives, these overnight trains produced engines not normally seen on daytime services. Newspaper trains, for example, were the last regular Class One workings for Class 40 locomotives.

As Intercity 125 High Speed Trains began replacing conventional locomotive hauled services from the mid-1970s, these trains were often the only ones where you could see a conventional, locomotive-hauled train at all. To anyone up and about late – or early – enough to travel on one, they looked and felt like a throwback to an earlier era.

Nor were night trains all about thundering expresses over busy main lines. Many secondary routes were operated by multiple-units through the day. But the first or last train could be just a couple of coaches and a locomotive – again sometimes of a type that rarely worked passenger services.

The main reason for this was that before British Rail began the long process of re-organising itself in the 1980s, many of these 'out of hours' trains performed two or three separate functions, carrying passengers, mail and sometimes newspapers too. For example, the first train of the day from Exeter to Barnstaple did exactly this, pausing at the unstaffed halt at Umberleigh simply to offload mail to a pair of waiting Royal Mail vans. The last train of the day from Dundee to Perth was a locomotive and two coaches because it would return in the early hours with mail and newspaper vans attached.

Freight has long been associated with overnight activity, but, as the traditional freight train – loose coupled and remarshalled every few miles – went into steep decline because journey times and costs had become so uncompetitive with road transport, British Rail fought back with a network called Speedlink, a service of overnight fast freight services that were deliberately run as block trains between two fixed points with only occasional pauses along the way to detach or pick up portions to allow the network to service more customers. Speedlink trains ran almost invariably by night and carried a wide range of commodities from chocolate to china clay. Ultimately, they proved a costly failure and even today the logistics and economics of persuading freight from road onto rail in significant quantities is a conundrum that has not been solved.

But how to capture them all on film? Today's digital cameras cope with low light levels quite easily. Colour film of the 1970s and 80s was a very different proposition. The only way to photograph night services was to catch them at rest – in a station platform, marshalling yard or wherever, and revert to the Victorian method of photography: the time exposure in which the shutter is held open for whole seconds at a time rather than just a tiny fraction, allowing the image to be recorded.

Even then, you cannot see the results immediately and do not have the comfort of the built-in light meter telling you that the exposure was more or less correct. So, having stayed up late and probably travelled a significant distance, you wanted to make sure that when the film arrived back from the processor, you had something to show for your efforts.

The answer was to take several shots of the same subject – a technique known as 'bracketing' - with experience being the only guide as to the range of exposures needed to be reasonably certain of getting at least one well-lit shot. An aid to this was to use an electronic flash to 'paint' in dark areas, with an assistant walking carefully around the edge of the framed shot to light up areas of heavy shade.

This was both time consuming and heavy on film! So a third requirement was to choose the subject carefully to try to ensure that if a technically acceptable picture did result, the subject matter would be worth the effort.

And there were the unexpected and unpredictable side effects of long exposures on the colour film of the day, and the way certain light sources would dominate a picture and, simply, the colour temperature of the available light: it might be a cold blue or a positively yellow, sodium type lamp, that was the only source of illumination.

Finally, there was the issue of gaining permission to be where members of the public are specifically excluded or not particularly welcome, setting up tripods and popping off flashguns. Often, thanks to the efforts of a good many British Rail and Royal Mail press officers, it was possible. In a handful of cases it was not. But for the record, it should be made clear that permission was sought – even to do pictures in public areas such as station platforms – before

work began. Train crew were asked permission before a flashgun was used, and a competent railway person was always present in potentially dangerous areas – which in practice meant anywhere trackside.

So, the traveller of forty years ago, impatiently waiting for a late evening train at York, Preston or Bristol, might have expected to see a lot of activity with mail trains being rapidly loaded and offloaded, lorries arriving with bundles of newspapers and just generally more trains around. Why has all this changed and why is the railway of tonight a much quieter place?

There are many answers. There are fewer sleeper trains because fewer people need to use them as daytime trains have become faster and more frequent. Now you can get from London to Leeds in two hours and Newcastle in three, why would you choose to travel on a sleeper? These days most people travel by car and the budget hotels that have sprung up at motorway service areas are the modern equivalent of the sleeper berth – though not so efficient because you cannot sleep and travel at the same time.

Newspaper trains fell victim to both the general decline in newspaper circulations and changing printing methods within the industry. The upheaval caused by News International's decision to shift production of *The Times*, *Sunday Times*, *Sun* and *News of the World* to Wapping lost BR about a third of its newspaper traffic at one fell swoop. Later, Mirror Group Newspapers ended their contract after demanding that BR take over responsibility for running the fleet of lorries that carried papers from printworks to railhead. BR was legally barred from operating such a road fleet even if it had wanted to. Another third of the traffic was lost, leaving behind a heavily loss-making service.

The end for all newspaper services came in 1988. The final customer was *The Financial Times*.

But even without these developments, it is unlikely that newspaper services could have survived much longer. Once virtually all national newspaper titles were printed in London, Manchester or Glasgow, carted from the printworks to the appropriate railhead and distributed nationwide. This is no longer the case. Today time is bought on many more presses in many more towns and cities. Printing plates can be transmitted electronically from a newspaper HQ to wherever the press happens to be located. This more diffuse system of production means that road distribution is the only really viable method of distribution.

Royal Mail had long had concerns about the reliability and punctuality of its dedicated services and several times during the 1980s announced plans to switch more mail from rail to road. It was a threat that BR's newly formed Parcels Sector fought back against, improving reliability and brining ingenuity to bear by creating a fleet of new, small parcels trains converted from redundant diesel multiple units made redundant by the fleets of Sprinter trains that were now appearing across the network. These had no secure guard's compartment and were thus unsuitable for carrying mail.

But the tide ran against mail by rail, and Royal Mail decided long before finally abandoning the railway that Travelling Post Offices, immortalised in films such as Night Mail had had their day. Human sorters cannot compare with the speed of machine-sorted mail, so the travelling post office would go and in its place would come a smaller network of trains carrying bulk mail, pre-sorted and ready for delivery at the destination.

Much investment went into a fleet of electric trains based on a four-car electric commuter unit and a network of dedicated mail terminals to get mail trains out of passenger stations. But even this slimmed down version collapsed in 2003 when Royal Mail could not agree terms with the privatised railfreight company English Welsh and Scottish Railway. It has since been revived, but on a far smaller scale than in the original plan and confined to only the West and East Coast Main Lines.

But it was British Rail's own attempts to reorganise itself that led to the withdrawal of the secondary trains, the multi-function services that made coy appearances at the beginning and end of the timetable, sometimes with journey times that the traveller had to check twice because they appeared so long – a reflection of the time needed to offload mail, newspapers and parcels en route.

In the 1980s BR abandoned its traditional geographical structure, based on regions, for one based on groups of services, known as sectors. For example, the Inter-City passenger business became a sector with one management team running the national express train network, rather than each region running its own services. The other sectors

included London and South East (later rebranded as Network South East), Parcels, Freight and, the Cinderella of the family, Other Provincial Services.

Other Provincial Services were the trains that nobody really wanted responsibility for: they were huge loss-makers and used old and inefficient equipment, some of it hand-me-downs from Inter-City. Fortunately, an energetic and talented management team gave OPS a makeover and it became Regional Railways, re-inventing the idea of secondary trains by investing in new fleets of 'Sprinter' type diesel multiple units and redrawing routes and timetables to meet changed travel patterns. But it spelled the end of the old multi-function train. As noted above, Sprinter trains simply were not configured for carrying mail, newspapers or parcels. And the handful of passengers wanting to leave Exeter for Barnstaple at 4am simply did not justify tying up expensive new assets in carrying so much fresh air around.

Taken together, all these factors amounted to the end of an era for the railways. A perfect storm of worn out equipment, changes to the way people and organisations ran their lives and a need to reorganise the railways themselves led to the changes that we see today.

Setting aside the separate arguments surrounding the benefits (or otherwise) of privatisation, some of the changes have clearly been for the better. In its final years British Rail demonstrated that abolishing regions and setting up sectors was absolutely the solution to cutting costs and increasing efficiency. The strides made by British Rail in the few years between this reorganisation and privatisation have been a hugely under-reported success story. But even success sometimes brings unwanted side effects and one of these is the way in which parts of the network now close down for much of the night either as an economy measure – to save staffing signalboxes for example – or to allow planned maintenance work to take place.

Operationally and financially this may all make perfect sense. But somehow it feels wrong that such a valuable asset as the national railway network cannot somehow be better used, as it once was, right around the clock.

Just as British Rail abandoned it's old structure, so does this book. Instead of the usual geographical tour of the network, it takes the reader on a chronological journey through the night, hour by hour, from dusk to dawn.

Some pictures *have* to be done by night. The final train left Clayton West for Huddersfield on January 24 1983 in the early evening. This meant that the Class 110 DMU that formed the last train left in darkness. The trackbed now hosts the Kirklees Light Railway, a narrow gauge steam powered line.

2000-2200

The now closed Manchester-Sheffield 'Woodhead Route' was operated by a fleet of unique 1500V DC electric locomotives known as Class 76 under the TOPS numbering system. Here, 76 054 backs onto 3E13, the Bolton-Peterborough parcels working, at Ashburys on the outskirts of Manchester. 76 054 would haul the train for only 40 miles or so before handing back to diesel traction at Rotherwood Sidings near Sheffield.

By mid-evening, the railway is beginning the metamorphosis into night mode. By day the other route linking Sheffield and Manchester, the Hope Valley line, was operated almost exclusively by multiple unit trains. But here, 31 110 prepares to leave Sheffield with 1M60 for Manchester Piccadilly, a train of loco hauled stock. The clouds of steam around the train are a reminder that carriage steam heating - a hangover from the days of steam locomotives - lasted into the 1980s and fleets of diesel locos needed expensive (and troublesome) boilers to provide it.

2000-2200

The Leeds-York service was another DMU stronghold, but by late 1982 the shift back to locomotive haulage was beginning and 31 424, a modified Class 31 with electric train heating equipment fitted, is ready to leave York.

At the other end of the country, a four-car Electric Multiple Unit pauses at Canterbury West station with the final train of the day. Nothing unusual - except that this was the last train before the start of one of the 1982 strikes in the dispute over 'flexible rostering' of train crew, something that today is just taken for granted.

Mail becomes an increasingly significant traffic as the evening wears on and here a Royal Mail van is having its contents transferred on the platform at Inverness station on May 5 1983.

At around the same time, but several hundred miles south, Class 47 loco 47 584 COUNTY OF SUFFOLK arrives at Harwich Parkeston Quay station with 1E87 Manchester Piccadilly-Harwich. This train was the direct descendant of the famous 'North Country Continental' service. With cheap air travel and Channel Tunnel rail services, the market for trains to service ferry departures has virtually disappeared.

A chilly late evening at Edinburgh Waverley and 37 017 waits with 1T03 to Glasgow Queen Street in May 1983. While many services on this route were locomotive hauled in daylight hours, a Class 37 was unusual power.

We tend to associate Travelling Post Office trains with high speed dashes through the depths of the night, but some of those on the fringes of the network started their journeys earlier. Nor were they always lengthy trains hauled by the most powerful locomotives. The Lincoln-Crewe TPO was almost always just two vehicles – the TPO itself and a van, referred to by the Royal Mail as a 'bag tender' – usually a GUV or BG. A Class 31 provided the modest power in this 1983 view at Lincoln.

Another little-known TPO was the Whitehaven-Huddersfield service – the only train of the day to directly link the two towns. It operated with one train running out and back and its primary function was to provide a series of connections between other TPO services along the route.

Perhaps not really a night picture at all, because DMUs handled all the traffic on the Sheffield-Huddersfield line (and still do). But this view of the final train of the day at Denby Dale is appealing because of the Christmas card effect of the snowfall which caused a significant amount of disruption in January 1983.

2000-2200

The railway's night shift really has begun with the change of shift at hundreds of signalboxes, stations and depots across the network. Here, the night shift signaller has just taken over at Cosford box. He will spend the next eight hours shepherding trains along the Telford-Birmingham route.

As the railway system moves further into the night, the long-distance services begin to make their moves. In the last years of the Travelling Post Office network, Royal Mail ran a train between Dover and Manchester. The Northbound working filled the departure platform at Dover with the Class 47 locomotive almost hanging off the platform end, so this wide-angle lens picture was the only way to capture it on film. The locomotive had recently been outshopped in the new 'large logo' livery.

Another picture that could only be taken by night: Class 76 locomotives 76 014 and 76 006 prepare to leave Barnsley Junction, Penistone, on July 17 1981 with the final haul of coal over the Woodhead Line. The electrics would take 6M50 to either Mottram or Godley Junction before handing back to diesel traction for the remainder of the run to Fiddler's Ferry power station. This picture sums up how times have changed over the past 35 years. The colliery, railway and power station have all closed as coal is phased out as a source of energy.

British Rail's sleeper network was once far more extensive than today's service. Back then, it was possible to get a sleeper from many northern towns and cities including Manchester, where 86 252 is caught standing at Piccadilly with the 1A01 overnight train to Euston.

But here is another part of the sleeper network that has survived the changes and cutbacks. The Euston-Fort William service is operated as a portion of the Inverness train and normally consists of three sleeping cars, a lounge car and some ordinary seated stock for those making a local journey. It is seen here on the southbound trip pausing at Crianlarich with a Class 37 locomotive at its head. The picture dates from August 1993.

Class 25 locomotive 25 069 stands at Chester waiting the
'right away' with 1J31, the last train of the day from Bangor
to Manchester.

As the clock creeps closer to midnight, parcels trains would appear in greater numbers, bringing locomotives to parts of the network where multiple unit trains normally ruled the roost. A class 31 stands at the head of 3A02, Bradford Exchange to Kings Cross.

At Kings Cross, you would have found a scene of activity with sleeper, parcels and mail services being readied for departure. Class 47 locomotive 47 207 has charge of 1N12 the Newcastle newspaper train in October 1982. Like mail, newspapers were treated as express passenger services, with 'Class 1' reporting numbers.

And next door, the roof of Barlow's famous train shed at St Pancras is shown to good effect, dwarfing the Class 47 locomotive standing at the head of the North Eastern TPO for Newcastle, running via Derby, Sheffield, Leeds and York.

Another sleeper service to survive is that from Paddington
to Penzance. These days it will be hauled by one of a trio
of Class 57 locomotives. 35 years ago it was Class 50 No.
50 014 WARSPITE waiting for departure from Paddington
with train 1B02.

At the far end of the original Great Western main line, at Bristol Temple Meads, 33 023 stands with train 1O99 to Southampton.

With overnight delivery being one of its key marketing points, the Speedlink freight network began a period of intense activity from mid-evening onwards. One important source of traffic was the Trafford Park industrial estate on the outskirts of Manchester. A pair of Class 76 electrics have just taken over the Trafford Park-Harwich service and will work it through to Rotherwood Sidings, Sheffield.

The only train of the day linking York and Shrewsbury was 1M41, the overnight mail service. Until its final years, this train also carried passenger accommodation and left York shortly after 10pm and reached Shrewsbury around 4am, with mail being sorted en route in two TPO vehicles. A veteran Class 45 locomotive, one of the first Modernisation Plan designs, 45 022 is in charge.

The postal trains network was designed to interconnect to a high degree, with mail being rapidly transferred between trains during station stops. At the same time that the Shrewsbury Mail is being prepared, the southbound North East TPO arrives at York, headed by 47 403. The wisp of steam reminds us that many TPOs were getting long in the tooth by this time and still required steam heat

The driver of 1M41 and his mate now wait for the transfer of mail to be completed and the 'right away' to Leeds, Huddersfield, Stockport and Crewe where connections with other mail services will be made.

Moving north, we find a Class 37 loco at Tyne Yard, about five miles to the south of Newcastle, with the 6S92 Hull-Aberdeen Speedlink service. The train paused here to detach the bulk cement tanks immediately behind the loco.

Tyne Yard was built as one of a national chain of hump shunting yards, designed to split up and remarshall freight trains as quickly as possible. But this type of general purpose freight train could not survive the onslaught of road transport with its greater convenience and cheaper cost. Tyne Yard adapted by serving the Speedlink network, but also by acting as a hub for local 'trip' freight workings. In these two views Class 31 31 301 is at the head of 8P13, the Tyne Yard-Tweedmouth trip while 37 068 has charge of a set of HBA hopper wagons on a service to Stella North power station. Both workings are long consigned to history.

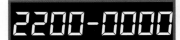

Another of the same chain of freight yards was Toton, sited on the Midland Main Line near Nottingham. A Speedlink service, train 6A83 to Willesden has 45 059 ROYAL ENGINEER standing at its head in March 1983.

The sleeper network used to include 'internal' Scottish services. An example was 1T04 the Inverness-Glasgow overnight train which is captured at Inverness with locomotive 47 517 at its head.

The flare from a signal light catches the flanks of 47 707
HOLYROOD at Edinburgh Waverley.

The Dundee-Perth route was normally operated by diesel multiple-units but the final train of the day from Dundee consisted of two passenger carriages and a locomotive which would return as the first train of the day from Perth with mail and newspaper vans. Class 26 loco 26 041 is waiting for the off with 1P23.

The Travelling Post Office network reached almost every part of the country, as evidenced by an unidentified Class 33 standing at Weymouth with the postal service to Waterloo.

One very seasonal night-time traffic was excursion trains to Blackpool for the autumn illuminations. In October 1983, 47 410 stands with 1T07 to Birmingham with the famous tower, suitably lit, in the background.

A Class 56 locomotive stands on the middle roads at Telford station with a train of cement powder tanks for Birmingham's Curzon Street depot in April 1984. One of BR's economy measures as its Government grant was repeatedly cut, was to close down signalboxes overnight, making the block sections longer. The train is waiting for a preceding service to clear the section ahead before it can be on its way.

And back at Dewsnap Sidings, Class 76s 76 010 and 76 016 are ready to leave with another Speedlink, this time for Severn Tunnel Junction.

2200-0000

Midnight on the railway of the 1970s and 80s. In this selection of views around the network we see (*clockwise from below left*) a Tinsley Yard Class 13 'master and slave' hump shunter 13 003 on the main hump; A view across the buffers at Manchester Piccadilly showing a variety of traction types; The West Coast Main Line at Crewe, looking south; A view inside Toton diesel depot; A view over the shunting hump at Toton Yard and semaphore signals at Dundee West.

Across the Pennines in Manchester, the newspaper traffic is building to a peak. The main newspaper service from Manchester Piccadilly was 1E62 to Grimsby. Until 1970 this service ran over the Woodhead Line, but by the time this early 1980s view was taken, it had been diverted via the Hope Valley to Sheffield and then on to Doncaster and Grimsby. The locomotive is 40 050. These newspaper workings were the last regular Class One trains that Class 40 locos could be seen on.

Most newspaper services used the city's Victoria station and a Class 40 locomotive is pictured here with 1E32, the Newcastle news. Bundles of papers had to be manually unloaded from lorries and onto trains. On some services the papers were then sorted while on the move – rather like TPO trains – making up batches for individual retailers to speed up distribution after the papers left the train. The rainy night only adds to the atmosphere.

Almost 200 miles to the south, Class 46 No. 46 031 stands at Kings Cross with 1L22, the Bradford News. Why send papers all the way from London? The reason is that some newspapers printed in London only, while others printed in both London and Manchester. Printing in Manchester gave a competitive edge – more copies could be run off and later news could be included.

A little further along the Euston Road, Class 86 locomotive 86 237 waits for the right away with 1G37, the Euston-Birmingham news.

At Waterloo, it has been a similar story: a string of departures for the south and south-west. Electro-diesel 73 156 stands at the head of 1W52, the Weymouth postal service in October 1982.

Mail, parcels and sleepers were two-way traffic and at Newton Abbot we see 50 029 on 1A05 the Plymouth-Paddington TPO service.

Much basic maintenance happened – and still does – overnight. The scene is Leeds Holbeck and Class 45 and 08 locomotives receive attention in the refuelling shed. The 45 had come off a south-west – north-east service.

Class 45 locomotives were true mixed-traffic units. Instead of a front line express passenger service, 45 015 has charge of 6V06 Speedlink service to Severn Tunnel Junction. It is ready to leave Toton in 1983.

One of the West Coast Main Line's fleet of AC electrics, 85 017 is caught at Carlisle with the Fort William sleeper. By this time – mid 1983 – the Class 85s had been ousted from most front-line duties and spent most of their time on empty stock and station pilot working.

And soon afterwards, 86 234 arrives with the Royal Highlander sleeper service to Inverness. There are now just two sleeper services per night leaving Euston, which divide at various points en route to serve Edinburgh, Glasgow, Aberdeen, Inverness and Fort William.

In addition to being a major passenger junction, Crewe was also an important interchange point for the Travelling Post Office network and an unidentified Class 47 stands with the 1V14 postal to Cardiff.

0000-0200

A batch of Class 46 locomotives could be found on and around the East Coast Main Line for many years and in this picture 46 028 earns its keep on 1N12, the London KX to Newcastle news. The picture was taken at Doncaster.

Back in Tyne Yard, 08 512 shunts chocolate vans onto 6S92, the Hull-Aberdeen Speedlink service which we met some time ago. Chocolate products from Rowntree's factories in York and Newcastle were an important source of traffic for the Speedlink network. It was the loss of this flow that prompted Railfreight to close Dringhouses Yard at York.

Parcels traffic criss-crossed the network right through the night and here a pair of Class 26 locomotives, 26 015 and 26 036 roll into Dundee station with the Aberdeen-Perth service.

Fixed formation trains led to a huge reduction in shunting movements on the daytime railway, but at night, parcels and mail workings still meant many complex carriage workings. Still at Dundee, the driver and his secondman wait patiently on 47 401 as mail and parcels are loaded on and off. Their train, 1N05 is also being combined with 1P04 for the remaining run north.

On the other side of the country, red signal lights stand guard on the main lines at Mossend Yard.

A pair of Class 33 locos, 33 004 and 33 021 provide the power for 1A69, the South Wales sleeper to Paddington as it pauses for a few moments at Port Talbot. The South Wales service was one of the many sleepers to be chopped in Inter-City's repeated economy drives.

Mossend was also a traction changeover point from electric to diesel and vice versa. 86 315 has just taken over the 1M16 Inverness-Euston working.

Class 47 locomotives were the staple power for TPO services simply because they were among the most reliable. One of the fleet coasts into Newcastle Central station with an unidentified working in 1984. The locomotive has been repainted in the 'large logo' livery while the TPO carriages themselves are in the process of being changed from BR's corporate blue and grey to the Royal Mail's own bright red and yellow.

Royal Mail sorters worked through the night on TPO trains. Some of them were rostered to work the full distance, lodging away from home and working back the following night. On other services there was a crew change halfway through the journey, so everyone arrived back at home in time for a good day's sleep. The working conditions were exactly as you'd expect from watching films such as 'Night Mail'... a swaying, rocking workspace with letters being expertly flicked into a score of pigeonholes, and plenty of tea!

Station stops were almost invariably rushed affairs: TPO trains were tightly timed and simply had to connect with each other. The alternative was hiring fleets of vans to take uncollected mail by road. When this happened, sorters would speak of the mail 'failing' and they took these failures almost personally. This is Crewe at around 2am.

The East Anglian Travelling Post Office, pictured behind the usual Class 47 locomotive is just a few moments away from departure time for London Liverpool St. Loading mail continued until the last minute.

As the night wears on, the last group of newspaper workings begin to depart, carrying Fleet Street's late editions and serving destinations closer to London. 31 416 stands at the head of 1K46, the Southend news, at Liverpool Street Station. The train is long gone and the station itself long since rebuilt.

And alongside, 37 110 is in charge of 1F40, the news to Witham.

Meanwhile, across London at Victoria station, the Dover news is about to begin its run. The locomotive is electro-diesel 73 017.

Also at Victoria is the Hastings news, this time with a diesel locomotive, 33 202 in charge. Locomotive hauled trains were a rarity during the day at Victoria. This one is particularly notable because the locomotive is one of the 33/2 sub-class, built to a narrower loading gauge than the main batch of Class 33s to allow it through the tunnels on the Hastings route. This line was suggested for closure when the special narrow stock built for it began to wear out. Ultimately, the solution was to single the tracks through the affected tunnels (they were built by an unscrupulous Victorian contractor), allowing the route to use standard rolling stock, and electrify it.

Night time also brought shunting locomotives into platforms normally monopolised by multiple-unit trains. 350hp Class 09 shunter 09 020 shunts vans at Victoria.

Much the same was happening at Kings Cross, where a pair of the ubiquitous Class 31 locos, 31 189 and 31 206, are providing the power for 1B22 the Peterborough news and parcels service.

Although air-braked Speedlink freight was seen as the future, the old-fashioned unbraked, or loose-coupled, freight was far from dead. Each train had to carry a brake van and Class 20 No. 20 168 has gone into the van siding at Toton Yard to collect one.

A major interchange point for the Travelling Post Office network was Derby and 45 076 is pictured heading south-west with 1V46, the Newcastle-Bristol TPO.

A class 31 loco, 31 111, is captured on film shunting vehicles from one TPO service to another at Derby. The sorting carriages themselves were rarely involved in these shunts, but vans of sorted mail (or mail waiting to be sorted) were switched from service to service as part of an intricate pattern of movements.

A TPO sorter at work. Until the network was finally closed in 2004, you could still post first-class mail into a red-painted letterbox on the side of each TPO. It would be hand-franked on the train, the last place where mail was franked manually rather than by an automatic sorting machine.

Trains carrying flasks of nuclear waste from power station to Sellafield, on the Cumbrian Coast Line, for reprocessing and storage are today still a source of freight traffic for the railway. In Tyne Yard, a Class 08 shunter gets to grips with a flask wagon. Nuclear traffic is one of the few remaining deemed to require a barrier wagon between the flask wagon and a locomotive. The barrier in this case is a redundant ferry van.

The main hump at Tyne was used only occasionally by 1983, but the secondary hump still saw some traffic and 08 254 sits just over the crest of the hump with the fan of sorting sidings and the lights of Newcastle visible in the background.

Class 31s were seen as a dependable maid of all work on what used to be the Eastern Region so it comes as no surprise to see 31 119 rostered to work 6E87 the Mossend-Parkstone Quay Speedlink service. It is about to restart after dropping a cut of wagons.

Across the other side of the country, and using electric rather than diesel power, 86 244 pauses at Carlisle with 1S04 – the Glasgow news. Several vans will be detached before the Class 86 heads into the night on the last leg of its journey.

Speedlink services were set up right across the BR network and 6D43, the Aberdeen-Mossend working, appears to be well loaded as it pauses in one of the platforms at Perth. The locomotive is 27 208, a class indelibly associated with Scotland for three decades or more.

Railway history lived on in the TPO network long after it had disappeared from daytime trains. Into the 1980s you could still find services named after long gone railway companies. There was a Great Western TPO and a North Eastern TPO on the network. Perhaps most surprisingly of all, was the Caledonian TPO, named after a railway company that disappeared in 1923! These two pictures show the Up working, train 1M49 behind 86 101 and the Down working, 1S58, headed by 81 012, both at Carstairs.

Edinburgh's English newspapers arrived on train 1G05, the
Carstairs-Edinburgh news which was a cut of vans removed
from the main Glasgow service. The crew pose obligingly in
the cab of 47 424 as unloading begins.

Wolverhampton in the early hours and 25 078 is waiting to move off with a single van of newspapers for Shrewsbury. Some of the contents will be transhipped at Shrewsbury onto the first train of the day over the Central Wales Line, so eager readers in Llandrindod Wells, Knighton and Builth Road will get their *Times* and *Sun*.

The news has arrived at Norwich Thorpe, and a Class 03 shunter, 03 180, complete with runner wagon to ensure that it operated all track circuits, is preparing to shunt the vans to release the train engine.

Job done and the Class 47 which has brought the news in from Liverpool Street waits at the platform end in a mist of diesel fumes. Someone has forgotten to switch marker lights for a tail light!

The first train of the day from Kings Cross to Leeds was once 1L01 and it recalled an earlier era of rail travel. The Class 31 locomotive was one of the pioneering Modernisation Plan designs of the 1950s. The pair of Mk I coaches provided for passenger use were corridor stock, with compartments instead of an open saloon. Steam heating was rapidly being phased out, but all these elements come together in the 04.30 departure. A Mk III air conditioned coach – part of a High Speed Train – can be seen behind 1L01 as it waits departure on May 5th 1982. It would take almost five hours to reach its destination – twice the time of daytime HSTs – stopping almost everywhere to offload mail, parcels and newspapers.

The news arrives at Yeovil: Class 33 loco 33 027 EARL MOUNTBATTEN OF BURMA stands in the dead-end platform at Yeovil Junction with 1V01 from Waterloo. The train also carried passengers and was the only service of the day to use this platform face, which had ended in bufferstops since the South Western Main Line was singled and downgraded in the 1960s. Happily, some of the damage has been undone. There are more double line sections and Yeovil Junction has been remodelled to bring both platforms back into regular use.

The final leg for some newspaper traffic was behind a diesel multiple unit. A three-car Class 110 unit arrives in Barnsley, with a single van which has been dropped at Sheffield by the Manchester-Grimsby train.

Mail trains began arriving at their destinations at the very end of the night, sorted bundles of mail now ready for delivery. This is 1M41, the York-Shrewsbury mail with locomotive 47 434 at the head.

You would normally travel on a multiple unit over the Exeter-Barnstaple line, but the first train of the day was locomotive-hauled, taking a couple of carriages and a string of vans to the market town. It paused at the unstaffed halt at Umberleigh where it was met by Royal Mail delivery vans. The locomotive is 31 113 and the date is May 1983.

Dawn is on its way as 47 362 waits for the right away in Mossend Yard.

Class 27 locomotive 27 051 stands at the head of the 6A17
Speedlink freight, also at Mossend.

A final view of Mossend with Class 37 No. 37 264 on the 6K22 trip working to Grangemouth.

Starved of investment for much of its life, British Rail became adept at making a little go a long way. At one point, its diesel-powered HST fleet was achieving better availability than French electrically powered inter-city stock. Part of the trick was concentrating maintenance work on the night shift so the maximum number of trains could be fielded each morning. One of the main centres for HST work was Leeds Neville Hill, which provided sets for the East Coast and Midland Main Lines. These pictures show HST sets being examined (*above*), washed (*right*) and fuelled (*left*), ready for the start of service.

Yeovil Junction signalbox at dawn. The railway begins a new day.